THE WORLD ART TOUR
Culinary Arts

Architecture
Clothing and Fashion
Culinary Arts
Dance
Decorative Arts
Drawing and Painting
Festivals
Sculpture

THE WORLD ART TOUR
Culinary Arts

BY Eric Benac

MASON CREST
Philadelphia • Miami

Mason Crest
450 Parkway Drive, Suite D
Broomall, PA 19008
(866) MCP-BOOK (toll free)
www.masoncrest.com

Printed in the United States of America

First printing
9 8 7 6 5 4 3 2 1

Series ISBN: 978-1-4222-4283-4
Hardcover ISBN: 978-1-4222-4286-5
ebook ISBN: 978-1-4222-7533-7

Cataloging-in-Publication Data is available on file
at the Library of Congress.

Developed and Produced by Print Matters Productions, Inc.
(www.printmattersinc.com)

Cover and Interior Design by Tom Carling, Carling Design, Inc.

CONTENTS

INTRODUCTION

This volume in The World Art Tour series explores the culture of cuisine. It focuses on different regions of the world and examines the essential food traditions of each region: Africa, Asia, Europe, Latin America and the Caribbean, the Middle East, North America, and Oceania. Of particular concern for each region is its history, traditions, religions, and cultural influences on the development of world cuisine. One might well ask why this topic is important enough to make it into a series on world art traditions. Can cuisine be an art? Does it showcase the development of cultures in the same way that literature, music, film, and television do? The answer is yes, absolutely! In fact, an argument could be made that you can learn more about a culture from its food than from its entertainment and history.

To help you better understand why this is true, each chapter of this book has been broken down into several sections. Longer sections provide an in-depth examination of the various factors that influence a society's cuisine. For example, you will learn about the origin of hummus, where couscous originated, and why your favorite Chinese restaurant serves such delicious food. Each of these sections focuses on specific elements and the factors that influence their development.

Mid-length pieces provide a shorter, but still educational, look at exciting elements of a cuisine and its development. Here you'll learn more about how climate affects cuisine development, the ways that the slave trade brought African food to the rest of the world, and how Cajun food got its start. Between the longer and the shorter pieces, you'll get the chance to watch an entertaining video that focuses on a visual representation of a critical point.

After the medium-length pieces, you'll read through shorter discussions that highlight essential aspects of a culture's cuisine. Expect to learn about how food can heal, how the United States has influenced cultures that once influenced it, and why food trucks have become so popular. All of these short pieces provide a fun but engaging look into the subject. In addition to these elements, each chapter includes a sidebar that provides more information on an interesting subject. All of this knowledge combines to create an engaging and unforgettable look at the world's cuisine, and you will come to understand why you eat so much corn, where tacos originate, and many other fascinating details and stories about the foods of the world.

WHY CULINARY ARTS ARE SO IMPORTANT

Before diving headfirst into the heavenly realm of world cuisine, it is important to touch on why this topic is so important to understand. First of all, a culture's cuisine provides insight into how the culture has developed over the years. For example, traditional Native American cooking focuses heavily on what the indigenous peoples of the continent could once hunt, gather, or grow. Bison, deer, and rabbit were the staple meats of Native Americans prior to the arrival of Europeans, and corn and potatoes were critical vegetables.

Does any of this food sound familiar to you? Many Americans still eat corn or potatoes nearly every day. These foods were not available to the European settlers who came to America, but they quickly became staple foods. After being shipped back to European shores, potatoes helped to fuel the continent's conquest of the world and even led to disasters like the Irish Potato Famine.

And that's just one example of how important food is to the development of a culture. Many others exist. For example, the prevalence of rice, vegetables, and smaller serving portions in Asian countries is a contributing factor to the slim physiques of the people in that region. The "all-you-can-eat" buffet is simply not a way of life for most people in Asia. As another example, the importation of coffee from India into Europe helped to fuel the Renaissance on the continent. Such facts showcase the importance of understanding the foods around you and where they originated.

One final example is the popularity of bananas around the world. Their initial discovery was in India in about 600 BCE, and the banana eventually became the first well-known international fruit. After being exported to the rich soils of South American countries in the fifteenth and sixteenth centuries, many European countries created companies to grow and sell this fruit. Sadly, the banana trade also caused wars between South American nations, which led to deaths and even revolutions that transformed the landscape of the continent forever. As you read this volume, you may well be pleasantly surprised, shocked, and even entertained by what you find. There's a good chance that you're going to learn things you never imagined about the food sitting on your plate right now. That's the beautiful thing about art: It transforms you and provides important knowledge about the world around you.

KEY TERMS

Charbroiling: Grilling (food, especially meat) on a rack over charcoal.

Acai: A South American tree that produces small berries used in many types of cuisine.

Afrikaners: A South African ethnic group descended from Dutch settlers.

Braising: A cooking method that fries food lightly and then stews it slowly.

Chili: A small hot-tasting pepper used chopped in sauces and spices.

Deseeded: Fruits or vegetables from which the seeds have been removed.

Halal: Religiously acceptable according to Muslim law.

Hummus: A spread made out of mashed chickpeas and other spices.

Farro: A food made from various types of wheats and prepared by cooking in water.

Fiber: A carbohydrate that cannot be digested.

Foodie: An individual who loves eating and trying new foods.

Imprint: Impress or stamp (a mark or outline) on a surface (such as the mind).

Indigenous: Originating or occurring naturally in a particular place, or being native to that place.

Jasmine rice: A long-grain rice grown primarily in Thailand.

Kebab: Cooked meat dishes that originated in the Middle East.

Kosher: Food satisfying the requirements of Jewish law.

Mole sauces: Traditional sauces originally used in Mexico.

Pilaf: A Middle Eastern or Indian dish of rice prepared in meat stock.

Pita: A flat, unleavened Middle Eastern bread that is often filled with various foods.

Pomegranate: An orange-sized fruit with a red skin and a sweet taste.

Quinoa: An ancient grain that originated in South America.

Sassafras: A North American tree with leaf extracts that can be used in culinary dishes.

Street food: Food prepared by vendors in an outdoor public location for quick consumption.

Tempura: A Japanese meal made of fish (or vegetables) fried in batter.

Turşu: A Middle Eastern word that means "sour."

Wok: A large pan in which stir-fry is prepared in many Asian cultures.

CHAPTER 1 AFRICA

African cuisine is rich in flavor, uses various native ingredients, and is as diverse as the continent is enormous. African food is also getting more popular throughout the world. If you've never tried it, you need to dig into some of the most delicious dishes available today.

COUSCOUS IS ALWAYS ON THE MENU IN NORTH AFRICA

Four countries make up the North Africa region known as the Maghreb: Algeria, Libya, Morocco, and Tunisia. The unique weather of the area, which ranges from the desert to a nearly tropical paradise, produces a broad array of ingredients, including seafood, lamb, beef, dates, olives, and many kinds of fruits.

Fans of Mediterranean cooking will be big on Maghreb cuisine, because its proximity to southern Europe has created a rich tradition of recipe swapping. That's why lamb, feta, and olives feature in so many Egyptian dishes. It's also why spices like ginger, cinnamon, parsley, and cumin are a part of so many incredible Maghreb dishes. Spice lovers will be delighted with the range of mouth-watering dishes available in the region.

A table filled with Maghreb cuisine, including a plate of couscous.

Shakshouka is scooped out of the skillet and eaten with a piece of bread.

Couscous serves as the staple for most Maghreb dishes. It is prepared in a pot known as a tagine, which is a glazed or painted pottery dish with a flat bottom, low sides, and a dome cover that creates a unique cooking style. As food cooks in a tagine, the dome collects and redirects condensation to the bottom of the pan. The design of the tagine has influenced the spicy cuisine of North Africa by concentrating spices and pepper juice at the bottom of the dish, so that the food soaks in this mixture.

The dishes of North Africa also include the following meals:

- *B'stilla*: This Moroccan meal includes meat, such as pigeon, chicken, or quail, spiced with sweet and sour flavorings. Each serving contains onions, saffron, coriander, almonds, and beaten eggs, all wrapped in a warqa pastry.

- *Shakshouka*: Originating in Israel and Tunisia, *shakshouka* (or *shakshuka*) is now eaten more heavily in North Africa. Ingredients such as chopped onions, chili peppers, cumin, and tomatoes are cooked on a stove in a skillet, in which two eggs are poached. Other flavorings are added after cooking, including chopped parsley.

- *Tajine*: Fans of chicken, lamb, and beef will fall in love with tajine (also known as tagine in some regions). Prepared in a tagine, from which the dish takes its name, this slow-cooked stew includes favorite meats topped with rich vegetables and dried fruit. Couscous or slow-cooked bread serve as the bed for this delicious meal.

WEST AFRICAN CUISINE: A DELIGHT FOR VEGETARIANS

The extreme climate variations in West Africa—including desert, semiarid or Sahel, savanna, and tropical forests—combined with its geography, has created a diverse array of cuisine cultures. Beyond that, West Africa was the region most affected by the slave trade of the 1700s and 1800s and also by European and American culture over the following years. Conversely, the slave trade spread West African cooking concepts and traditions more rapidly around the world than other types of African cuisine.

For example, the tomatoes, corn, plantains, peanuts, and chili peppers common in many West African recipes were brought to the area by slave traders and explorers. At the same time, slave ships then carried African foods, such as black-eyed peas and okra, back to Europe and America, and the slaves brought their food traditions with them.

A plate of jollof rice is seasoned with chilies and tomatoes.

Fufu is made by boiling starchy foods. It is then pounded with a large wooden mortar and pestle into a pasty mass ready for cooking.

In spite of this exchange of ingredients, almost no European or American influence can be found in the preparation methods of West African cooking. For example, many West African dishes are roasted over a fire in a simple skillet and prepared with vegetables such as onions, tomatoes, hot peppers, and okra. Native oils, such as palm oil or shea butter, are used to grease the pan and prevent burning. Expect peanuts and other root vegetables in the average West African meal, including these dishes:

- **Jollof rice**: This rice staple is cooked slowly in a large pot and liberally mixed with peanuts, tomatoes, chilies, and very little meat.

- *Fufu:* Staple foods in Africa don't come any simpler than *fufu*. It consists of a starchy vegetable that has been cooked and turned into a pasty mass. *Fufu* is then dipped in a stew and swallowed whole.

- **Groundnut stew**: Stews in West Africa consist mostly of vegetables or nuts—just as this dish does. It includes peanuts, tomatoes, and onions, and it pairs well with *fufu*.

SOUTH AFRICA'S EXCITING MELTING POT OF CONFLICTING CULINARY POSSIBILITIES

The history of South Africa has long been one of unfortunate oppression and painful reconciliations. European settlement of the area began in the 1600s when the Dutch, and later the French and Germans, invaded and took control of the area, which they retained for hundreds of years. Beyond European lifestyles, religions, and ideas, they brought with them a variety of foods and culinary influences.

Biltong *hangs and dries in the sun before being eaten.*

However, native cooking influenced the Europeans just as much as the Europeans affected the native population. As a result, a unique style of South African cooking—known as Afrikaans cuisine—developed. Most South African dishes follow this tradition and include a lot of dried meats, such as *biltong*, a type of jerky, and *droewors*, a dried sausage. These foods contain excessive levels of salts and preservative spices.

Typical Afrikaans dishes contain red meat, potatoes, rice, and vegetables flavored with butter and sugar. *Braai*, or barbecue meat, consists of spiced sausage, kebabs, and steaks cooked over hot coals. Side dishes, such as bread rolls and salads, were designed to be simple so they could be eaten while on the go. All of these foods were influenced not only by the tropical to temperate climate of South Africa but also by the tough on-the-go style of settlement common in the early colonial period. There was no time to preserve food, so dishes had to be easy to make and quick to eat.

Traditional South African cuisine—which is separate from the Afrikaans style—consists of the foods of multiple subcultures, including Sotho, Tswana, Xhosa, and Zulu dishes. Like Afrikaans dishes, most traditional South African food is easy to prepare and quick to eat. However, it consists mostly of locally grown crops and varies depending on food availability. Maize (corn), rice, potatoes, leafy vegetables, and meat from livestock form the basis of most South African dishes.

Here are some traditional South African dishes:

- *Bobotie*: A mixture of spiced meat, egg toppings, raisins, and sultanas. This dish is served at dinner either as a vibrant and sweet appetizer or as a main dish.

- *Potjiekos*: In this dish, locally prepared meat and vegetables are cooked in a large cast-iron pot over a fire. The ingredients, such as lamb, ginger, bay leaves, onions, carrots, and garlic, provide the flavoring and spice.

Potjiekos *cooks over an open flame in a cast-iron pot.*

- *Chakalaka*: This soupy stew includes peppers, carrots, tomatoes, relish, and other types of locally grown vegetables. It pairs well with *boerewors*, a variation of *droewors* that are thinner and more heavily dried.

The Yam Festival

Yams might not inspire excitement in the average person, but they are a staple vegetable in Africa and have served as one of the continent's most essential foods for centuries. That's why, every year, the Yam Festival celebrates this delicious food.

Typical celebrations of the festival include drumming, yam preparation, and a variety of other rituals that celebrate the yam as a vital source of life. Delicious yam-based meals like yam *fufu* (mashed yams flavored with plantains) are prepared and served among various tribes and in many cities. The Yam Festival is an intense and critical celebration that provides Africans with a source of excitement every year.

CENTRAL AFRICA: A SPICY CENTER FOR MOUTH-WATERING CUISINE

Movies and television shows often portray Africa as a desert wasteland, but most of the continent is in fact tropical. And fewer areas are more tropical (or hotter) than Central Africa. It is here that one finds some of the spiciest foods in the world, and the imported hot pepper remains a favorite in this region for a variety of reasons.

First of all, the tropical climate provides the perfect growing environment for hot peppers. Secondly, hot foods create a potent flavor and provide benefits, such as causing increased sweating or acting as a decongestant, which make them useful for tropical climates. Dishes like hot pepper soup, *doro wat* (whole chicken stewed in peppers), and Ethiopian cabbage dishes all tap into these spicy flavors.

Hot weather also influences cooking methods in this region, such as the use of the tagine. The tagine's use of concentrated heat focuses high temperatures in a concentrated area and minimizes temperature increases in the average Central African home.

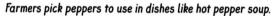

Farmers pick peppers to use in dishes like hot pepper soup.

VEGETABLES ARE KING IN EAST AFRICAN CUISINE

East African countries, such as Burundi and Eritrea, are very mountainous and difficult to explore and settle. However, the brave native peoples of the area have crafted a cuisine all their own by focusing on growing hardy vegetables in this challenging landscape. For example, Burundian cuisine includes ingredients like corn, beans, and manioc, plants that are easy to grow in just about any region.

In Ethiopia, which is a little less mountainous and contains many rivers, dishes such as *wat* are popular. This meaty stew uses beef, the most popular red meat in the region, and multiple types of vegetables to create a vibrant mix of ingredients served over *injera*, a sourdough flatbread.

The heavy emphasis on root vegetables and other kinds of plants in the region makes East African foods some of the healthiest in the world. As a result, residents of the area are typically quite slim and healthy, though, unfortunately, diseases such as sleeping sickness shorten the average life span in the region to just over 51 years.

An Ethiopian woman tills her land, prepping it for various root vegetables.

HOW THE SLAVE TRADE INFLUENCED THE SPREAD OF AFRICAN CUISINE

By all accounts, the European slave trade was the worst thing to happen to the African continent in its long history. It pitted tribe against tribe, opened the continent up to European domination, and set development back for centuries. However, the slave trade was also crucial to spreading African foods around the world, and it influenced the development of many traditional African dishes that are still eaten today.

For example, the slave trade brought coffee, watermelon (and many other types of melons), okra, and black-eyed peas to Europe and America. Africans bought and sold as slaves brought their traditional recipes to new lands and inspired cuisines as diverse as Cajun cooking and Southern soul food in the United States, as well as many dishes in the Caribbean. For example, the popular Caribbean dish callaloo, a meal with leafy greens and okra, comes directly from Africa.

It is sad that such a destructive force spread these foods around the world, but recent trading between Africa and the rest of the world has helped to spread this influence even further. In just one of many examples of this influence, Asian countries that use jasmine rice in their meals do so because of its import from the African region.

Watermelon, and many other types of melons, are a staple food in Africa. They were brought to Europe and America by slave traders.

DON'T LIKE AFRICAN FOODS? THESE DISHES MIGHT CHANGE YOUR MIND

African meals might seem impossibly ethnic or outside of your taste range, but you probably love foods that come from the region without realizing it. For example, if you have ever enjoyed a delicious curry over a bed of chopped chicken and couscous, or bunny chow—a hollow loaf of bread filled with a lamb or beef curry—you are enjoying African cuisine. Fans of beef jerky should try biltong, a dried meat that is common throughout many regions in Africa. And if you've ever had a flatbread pizza, you are enjoying a dish found in many restaurants and homes throughout Africa.

Bunny chow.

STREET FOOD IS A WHOLE NEW WORLD IN AFRICAN CUISINE

Like in many continents of the world, street food is tremendously popular in Africa. The busy and bustling streets of the average African metropolis are filled every day with busy vendors selling traditional favorites like sardines spiced with chili, tomato, pepper, and lemon juice. These dishes are popular in cities because they provide a little extra energy to handle life in a bustling metropolis.

In rural areas, one can still find many street food vendors selling dishes like *dholl puri*, a type of stuffed bread filled with split peas and curry, as well as a variety of delicious kebabs, sirloin steak chunks, boiled chicken breasts, and even young coconuts. Local herbs and spices, such as peppers, are often used in these dishes as a curative for various diseases.

Street food cooks prepare seafood in Zanzibar, Tanzania.

CONTEMPORARY CHANGES IN AFRICAN FOOD CONTINUE TO INFLUENCE ITS DEVELOPMENT

As Africa has developed as a continent, its traditional food has changed to stay modern. For example, it isn't uncommon to see multiple McDonald's restaurants spread through the average African city. Don't fret, though— this Western influence is tempered by the proud traditions of African cuisine. For example, common African ingredients like okra and olives top many dishes in McDonald's and similar fast-food restaurants.

McDonald's restaurants are found all over Africa these days.

Like other cultures around the world, African cultures synthesize new cuisine concepts and adapt them to traditional cooking methods. In this way, new and exciting variations come out of the continent every year and continue to influence culinary experiences around the world.

An herbalist sells a variety of ingredients for home remedies.

IS YOUR BACK SORE? AN AFRICAN DISH MIGHT HELP

Africans have always been in touch with the potential healing powers of food. For example, they have used foods like yams for generations as a healing tool for various health problems. And the potent chili peppers common in the region are often used as a powerful aphrodisiac or put in pain-reducing compounds. This use of food is not superstitious but has a real basis in science. For example, plants such as gum arabic are used to treat bronchitis, diarrhea, and other types of disease. Studies have shown that many of these natural remedies do have positive effects on different kinds of sicknesses.

CHAPTER 2 ASIA

Asian cuisine is probably the most famous of all ethnic food types, having been spread around the world by immigrants sharing their proud culinary heritages. From hand-rolled sushi to delicious sesame chicken and unbeatable pho soup, there's a lot to love. Traditional Asian cuisine, however, is a little different from what the average person might expect.

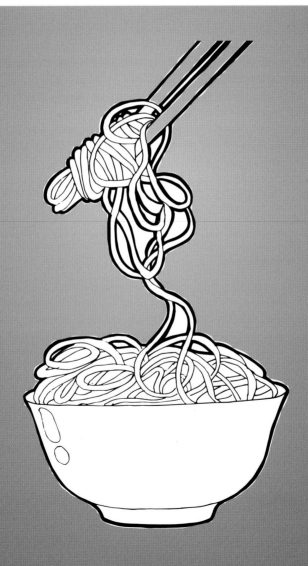

CHINA: EIGHT REGIONS, EACH WITH A UNIQUE CULINARY IDENTITY

Traditional Chinese food comes from eight different cultural regions, each with its own unique character and flavor profile:

- **Canton**: Mild and slightly sweet, with spices or sauces used only to enhance the natural taste of the ingredients.
- **Sichuan**: Spicy and heavily seasoned, typically with fennel, pepper, and cinnamon.
- **Zheijang**: Strong emphasis on seafood, bamboo shoots, and very salty tastes, due to the region's proximity to the ocean.
- **Fujian**: Focuses heavily on slightly sweet and sour soups, in which seafood and river fish are main ingredients.
- **Jiangsu**: Uses lots of seafood and vegetables prepared in elaborate stews and braises, which are creatively presented.
- **Hunan**: Incredibly spicy cuisine, which is warming during the region's extremely cold winters.
- **Anhui**: Hearty dishes made with foods that are easy to find in this mountainous region.
- **Shandong**: This coastal region prefers seafood prepared simply, such as braised. It also uses noodles made of wheat rather than rice, because the area grows a lot of wheat.

Many of the spices and ingredients used in these cuisines are chosen because of their healing properties, which have long been known in traditional Chinese

What Is American Chinese Cooking?

If you were to take your favorite dish from a Chinese restaurant back to China, the residents would scarcely recognize its flavor. That's because American Chinese food is a unique creation with a history that began in the late 1880s and expanded to become more prominent throughout the twentieth century.

During this period, most Chinese cooking was very traditional, but canny restaurant owners noticed that it tasted too foreign and unfamiliar to Americans. So Chinese chefs removed some of the harsher ingredients and then added sweeter sauces and more meat. Voilà! American Chinese cuisine was born.

medicine (TCM). Ginger, garlic, and asparagus, for example, are used in many dishes as a way of promoting health.

Most Chinese meals include rice. In fact, the Chinese word for rice is *fan*, which also means "meal." The average Chinese person eats rice multiple times a day and combines it with various foods, such as dried or baked seaweed. Rice is eaten so regularly in China (and other areas of Asia) because it grows abundantly and is inexpensive to harvest and prepare.

People take cooked food from the hot pot.

Vegetables are also an essential part of the Chinese diet, and bean sprouts, cabbage, and ginger root are used in every region. Vegetables are abundant, less expensive than meat, and often easier to prepare. Ingredients are combined into a one-pot dish, flavored with a soy-based sauce, and eaten with white rice. In fact, soybean curd (tofu) is commonly used as a meat substitute for the health-conscious population. Popular dishes in China include a variety of ingredients and cooking methods, such as the following:

- Peking duck, which is served with a hearty side of vegetables

- Jellyfish, which is usually deep-fried

- Chicken feet, which can be deep-fried or stir-fried

A chef prepares Peking duck.

- *Chow fun*, a noodle dish made with stir-fried meat or seafood and bean shoots

- Hot pot, a cooking method that includes a bowl of simmering soup stock into which different ingredients are added, such as meat, vegetables, mushrooms, and tofu

- Sea cucumbers, which are stir-fried with winter melon, *kai-lan* (Chinese broccoli), shiitake mushrooms, and cabbage

Preparation methods vary depending on the region. For example, Jiangsu cooking uses a complex simmering and braising method that takes more skill than the stir-frying techniques common in Canton. Methods also vary depending on the ingredients available in a particular region. For example, Peking duck prepared in Shandong contains dark meat, pancake wraps, and a sprinkling of scallions. In Anhui, however, it includes vegetables, such as green beans, that are common to the area.

JAPAN: ROOTED IN TRADITION AND SURROUNDED BY THE SEA

For thousands of years, Japan was a closed country that did not welcome outsiders. Although the nation has opened up to the rest of the world over the past century, that history of isolation created an insular cuisine that is very different from the rest of the Asian countries.

For example, much of the island nation's traditional food preparation focuses on raw seafood. One of its most famous and ancient dishes is sushi, which is raw (and sometimes fermented) fish served on fermented rice (fermentation preserves its freshness). These days, high-end sushi restaurants hire celebrated chefs who slice the raw fish right in front of you and prepare it with ingredients like carrots, vinegared rice, cabbage, and much more. Training to be a master sushi chef takes at least five to 10 years, and great emphasis is placed on learning to safely prepare raw food.

What is interesting about Japanese cuisine in America is that it has retained its traditional flavor. For example, sashimi (thinly sliced raw food, such as fish, beef, or chicken) is prepared in the same way in Tokyo as it is in New York City, although raw chicken is not often on Japanese American menus because of fears of contamination with bacteria such as salmonella, which can cause severe illness. Different regions in Japan have their own variations of sushi, as follows:

- **Makizushi**: Rice and ingredients are rolled in nori seaweed, with sesame seeds and fish eggs on the outside.
- **Gunkan maki**: Invented in the 1940s, this variation includes nori seaweed topped with urchin, squid, roe, and potato salad.
- **Temaki**: A conical type of sushi that is easy to make at home and in restaurants, temaki typically includes squid, shiso leaves, and more.
- **Narezushi**: This variety, which uses fish preserved in salt for several months or years, is very sharp in flavor.
- **Nigiri**: The most commonly eaten type of sushi around the world, nigiri is easy to prepare and includes seafood, veggies, meat, and tofu.
- **Oshizushi**: Unlike other types of sushi, this variety is pressed and layered with other ingredients, such as bamboo leaves.
- **Sasazushi**: This variation omits the seaweed and instead wraps the ingredients in bamboo leaves. The inside often includes bamboo shoots, mushrooms, and salmon.
- **Temari**: More popular in Japanese homes than in restaurants, this type uses a ball of rice topped with thin layers of fish and vegetables.

Different than the typical sushi roll, temari is a ball of rice topped with layers of fish and vegetables.

These dishes are often Americanized in subtle ways. For example, although cooked chicken is frequently used in Japanese restaurants in the West, it is not common in Japan. And if you ask for California rolls in Japan, most sushi chefs are going to be confused. However, American favorites like fried tempura are just as popular in Japan. Tempura consists of fish, shrimp, and other types of seafood, as well as vegetables, that are battered and deep-fried. The batter is kept cold before the seafood and vegetables are dipped in it. This step creates the uniquely fresh, crispy texture of tempura.

The country's relatively new openness to outside influences has fueled the progression from traditional to modern Japanese cuisine. Appealing to broader tastes has become more important than focusing strictly on tradition. Still, most dishes in Japan are the same as they were during imperial times, which sets them apart from the cuisine of other Asian countries.

Restaurant goers enjoy a fresh batch of seafood tempura.

THAILAND: SPICE AND RICE

Thai cuisine is one of the hottest in the world. Thailand's tropical climate is ideal for growing a large number of chilies, and residents also import hot spices from neighboring India to create the blazing hot taste profile of Thai food. Here's a fun fact: Thailand is the world's second largest exporter of rice (only India surpasses it). Rice is so prevalent in Thailand that the phrase for "I'm hungry" literally means "I want to eat rice." Jasmine rice is the most popular type in high-end restaurants. For those who cannot afford it, *khao soi* rice is a less expensive alternative. The average person in Thailand eats about a half a pound of *khao soi* daily.

Thai dishes are prepared with multiple spices, such as garlic and chili, which are often complemented with basil, peanuts, potatoes, and even coconut. Other ingredients include fish, pork, chicken, beef, onions, broccoli, bamboo shoots, bell peppers, shallots, eggplant, bean sprouts, carrot, kale, and cabbage.

*A chef prepares a large pot of **tom yum goong** at a street fair.*

A very popular dessert item in Thailand is mango sticky rice.

Seasonal availability often comes into play. During the monsoon season, for example, it can be hard to find vegetables, including various types of broccoli. Internationally popular Thai noodle dishes, such as pad Thai, are also a staple of most Thai diets. These noodles are made out of rice, eggs, or mung beans (the source of bean sprouts). Peanut sauces are often paired with pad Thai as a milder complement to spicier dishes in a meal.

A few of the popular dishes enjoyed in Thailand include *tom yum goong*, a spicy shrimp soup; *som tum*, a sour and spicy green papaya salad; *gaeng som pak ruam*, a vegetable soup with curry; and *larb moo* (also known as *laab moo*), a minced pork salad served on top of rice. Raw vegetable salads mixed with lime, fish sauce (made from fermented fish), and chili are also a favorite. And Thai people love egg-based desserts made with rice, coconut milk, sweet corn, or kidney beans. These traditional meal-enders are often served alongside modern Western treats, such as cake and ice cream.

KOREA: KIMCHI, THE ULTIMATE PROBIOTIC

Traditional Korean cuisine focuses on rice, a simple stew, and a few side dishes. From this primary jumping-off point, there are nearly endless variations. Expect ingredients like beef and cabbage alongside flower leaves, jellyfish, and pickled vegetables. The more straightforward and less decorative nature of Korean food has made it a popular alternative to Chinese, Japanese, and Thai cuisines. The basic seasonings of Korean foods stem from the simple agrarian lifestyle prevalent in the country in its early years. Common seasonings include red pepper, garlic, ginger, and mustard seeds.

One of the most popular traditional dishes in the country is kimchi. This fermented-cabbage preparation includes peppers, ginger, scallions, and much more. It is incredibly spicy and is often paired with a simple beef stew to round out the meal. In recent years, a strong case has been made for the health benefits of probiotic foods. Kimchi, which is salted and fermented with live bacteria, could be thought of as the ultimate health food.

Bibimbap is another traditional Korean dish that has gained an international following. A utilitarian one-dish meal, it consists of rice, seasoned vegetables, mushrooms, beef, chili pepper, soy sauce, and a fried egg mixed in a large bowl. The ordinary working person in Korea often eats this dish because it provides a healthy mix of hearty ingredients on the go.

An annual Kimchi Making and Sharing Festival is held annually in Seoul, Korea.

LAOS: A LANDLOCKED NATION THAT LOVES ITS VEGGIES

Landlocked Laos is often forgotten when it comes to Asian cuisine. Recently, however, more and more people are learning to love the country's vegetable-rich foods, which are naturally low in fat and cholesterol. And if you don't like fish, you're in luck—Laotian cuisine features very little seafood.

Sticky rice, or *khao niaw*, is one of the staple foods of the country. Commonly served in a small bamboo basket, sticky rice is often paired with *larb*, a minced-meat salad that is the country's unofficial national dish. *Larb* mixes meat, such as duck, pork, fish, chicken, and beef, with fish sauce, ground rice, chili peppers, and fresh herbs.

As for soups, *khao piak sen* is one of the most popular. It consists of chewy rice noodles mixed with pork, chicken, shallots, garlic, coriander leaves, bean sprouts, and lemongrass. These three dishes are staples of most Laotian's diets and are well worth trying.

Khao niaw *is a popular dessert in Laos.*

VIETNAM: PHO AND BANH MI IS SOUP AND A SANDWICH

Although the lengthy Vietnam War held this country back from modernization for at least a decade, it has recently and rapidly become integrated into the rest of the world. A new wave of immigrants from Vietnam has spread its cuisine beyond its borders, making new fans all around the world. Pho soups are the best known and most popular foods in the country. These soups consist of pho rice noodles flavored with beef, chicken, bean sprouts, cilantro, onions, basil, chili, and fish sauce.

These tastes mix to create an unforgettable one-pot meal. The popularity of this dish is due to its ease of cooking—which suits the life of the average agrarian Vietnamese peasant—and the way it can be eaten while on the go. *Banh cuon* is another dish that has become an international favorite and is often paired with *banh mi. Bahn cuon* is a delicate wide sheet of steamed fermented rice batter flavored with vegetables, meat, or even a light curry spread, whereas bahn mi is a sandwich similar to a baguette, which showcases the French influence on the region. And no traditional Vietnamese meal is complete without summer rolls, which are made of greens and a protein such as shrimp or pork wrapped in a translucent rice pancake. The roll is dipped in peanut sauce and makes for a tasty treat.

A woman serves pho to restaurant patrons.

HEALTH BENEFITS OF ASIAN FOOD

The Asian diet provides a number of health benefits tied to longevity.

The majority of people in Asian countries are either at a healthy weight or under-weight, largely due to the foods they eat. Many of these dishes provide a variety of health benefits. Some of the health advantages associated with Asian foods include lower cholesterol levels, lower incidence of type 2 diabetes, lower risk of heart disease, and weight loss and weight stabilization. That said, there are also a few health problems associated with the Asian diet, including an excess of sodium and a focus on white rice. By minimizing the amount of salt (and soy sauce) and switching to brown rice, however, one can make Asian meals even healthier.

SPICE IS VERY NICE IN INDIA

No list of Asian foods would be complete without the hot, hot, hot world of Indian cuisine. After all, this is the country that invented curry! Cooking lamb, chicken, and vegetables in this delicious hot sauce is an Indian tradition. Curries get their kick from dried or fresh chilies, which are combined with herbs and spices such as coriander, cumin, and turmeric. Curry powder, by the way, is largely a Western invention dating back to the eighteenth century. It's a premixed powder of spices, but in India both chefs and home cooks prefer to mix their own blend of spices. The robust flavors and spici-ness of Indian food is an important part of Indian culture. This cuisine is said to purge the body and the mind of negative thoughts and to improve physical health.

An Indian street vendor cooks with curry.

STREET FOOD IS FAST FOOD ALL OVER ASIA

Steamed dumplings are a favorite street food in Hong Kong.

Most Asian countries are densely populated, with the majority of people living in cities. This unique situation has created a strong culture of street food in just about every part of the continent. This type of food is fast, nutritious, and inexpensive to make. For example, street vendors can serve busy workers a quick bowl of rice, tofu, and vegetables as they go to or leave work for the day, or as they take a break for lunch. Street foods are designed to be easy to make and quick to eat. In Vietnam, pho soups, rich in flavor and nutrients, are available on every street corner. *Panipuri*, a favorite in India, consists of small deep-fried bread bowls filled with potatoes, chickpeas, chili, chutney, and other ingredients. In Hong Kong, fried or steamed dumplings filled with meat or vegetables are just the thing for hungry people on the go.

TIPS ON COOKING ASIAN DISHES

Asian dishes are fun to prepare, but some dishes take a bit of know-how to get right. Here are some helpful hints that will make the process easier and the food even better.

- Vary the sauces you use. When cooking Asian meals, try to use different types of sauces to create a more diverse and engaging range of dishes.
- Woks are crucial. Woks are necessary for Asian cuisine because they allow the ingredients to be cooked quickly and evenly, while keeping them as crispy as possible.

An expert cooking tip: Use multiple woks!

- Dump the white rice. Brown rice may take longer to cook, but it is far healthier than white rice. It should be substituted into as many meals as possible.
- Don't ignore zero-calorie noodles. There are many types of starch-based Asian noodles available that have no calories but are still abundant in a multitude of vitamins and minerals.
- Marinate your meat. Marinating fresh meat before cooking Asian food will ensure that the meat is saturated with flavor.

CHAPTER ③ EUROPE

You might think that you know European cuisine like the back of your hand, or you might even think these foods are just boring. If so, you're missing out on diverse cuisines and cultures that vary wildly from one side of the continent to the other. Frankly, European cuisine is much more interesting than most people realize.

IF YOU LOVE MEAT, GERMANY HAS GOT YOU COVERED

If there is one ingredient that characterizes German cooking, it is pork. Germany is the largest pork producer in the European Union, with more than 5.5 million tons of it processed in 2017 alone. The country's pork production is third only to China and the United States, and this considerable emphasis on raising pigs has been a tradition in the country, particularly in the northwest, for centuries.

That tradition has made the German pork industry the best in the world. Every element of production, from breeding to slaughtering to pest control, helps to create some of the most delicious and high-quality pork in the world. And with typical German efficiency and creativity, the country's pork dishes have inspired generations of taste buds and dozens of cuisine cultures around the world.

A butcher shop in Germany.

BAUERN-KNACKWURST 1.29

BIER-SCHINKEN 1.59

LEBER-KÄSE 1.19

JAGD-WURST 1.19

LACHS-SCHINKEN 2.19

SCHINKEN-ROTWURST 1.69

LEBER-ROTW

For example, pork sausage originated in Germany, and it is still one of the staples of most modern meals. Rouladen—a slice of pork wrapped around bacon, pork belly, chopped onions, pickles, and mustard—remains one of the most popular dishes in the country. Rouladen is often delivered with a side of thick noodles mixed with dumplings and served in a thick pork broth. Fried carrots, potatoes, turnips, and broccoli covered with hollandaise sauce also serves as a delicious side dish.

All of the foods in these dishes are native to Germany, and the ingredients grow there in abundance, thanks to the country's rich agricultural tradition. The sometimes cold climate has also influenced German cuisine to include cabbage in just about every dish. German sauerkraut was invented as a delicious way of pre-serving cabbage during the region's often harsh winters. And the more than 1,200 breweries in the country are part of the same tradition—drinking beer helps warm the blood and increase circulation in extreme weather conditions.

Rouladen is made by wrapping pork around bacon, chopped onion, pickles, and mustard.

RUSSIAN CUISINE: DIVERSE AND FLEXIBLE

Talking briefly about Russian cuisine is difficult due to the uniquely massive size of this country. At one point, Russia contained 11 time zones (just shy of half the world), and its culture is likewise diverse. The western portion has foodstuffs similar to Poland and other nearby countries, but the south and west have cuisines that are closer to Asian styles.

One major unifying factor in Russian cuisine is the influence of the Orthodox Christian religion. Even during the anti-religious days of Communism, beliefs remained strong among most residents of the country. Therefore, Russians often go through a variety of fasts, including during Easter and Christmas, and these influence their cuisine. However, the most significant influence on traditional Russian cuisine is the agrarian nature prevalent in the nation for most of its history.

The diverse range of foods grown or foraged in Russia's many fields include tomatoes,

Svekolnik takes on a pink hue when beet juice is mixed with sour cream and yogurt.

A woman rolls dough to make dumplings.

mushrooms, cucumbers, berries, wheat, barley, and much more.
Favorite meats include beef, pork, lamb, and fish and caviar is also popular. Soups and stews combining many of these ingredients remain staple foods. Cold Russian soups are known as borscht and consist of varieties like *botvinya* (beets, sorrel, dill, and cucumbers) and *svekolnik* (beet juice, sour cream, and yogurt).

Many of Russia's traditional dishes were adjusted to meet the ideological demands of the Soviet Union in the early twentieth century. In many cases, meals were simplified to make them more pragmatic and easier to prepare. For example, dishes such as Olivier (or Russian salad) focused on peasant-grown foods served with staple meats or fish, such as herring. Fare that was considered bourgeois or fancy, such as most types of European-style cakes, were banned in favor of chicken noodle soups, rich cabbage-based salads, and regional favorites like dumplings, shashlik (Russian sausages), and beef Stroganoff.

FRENCH CUISINE IS A WORLD FAVORITE

France has led the European cooking world for centuries, but that wasn't always the case. During the early 1400s through the 1600s, the French were influenced heavily by Italian cuisine styles of the time. By integrating many Italian cooking methods into traditional French techniques, the country transformed its cuisine culture into one of the best and most diverse in the world.

That diversity isn't just a result of the Italian influence, however. France has a unique combination of climate types, including continental, oceanic, and Mediterranean. Western France's position on the Atlantic Ocean leads to plenty of rainfall and cold, but rarely snowy, weather. The Eastern continental region shares warm summers and cold winters with its German neighbors. To the south, the Mediterranean region is hot and has mild winters with little rainfall.

A pot of coq au vin simmers on the stovetop.

A tarte tatin is ready for the oven.

As you might imagine, these climates have greatly influenced French cuisine. For example, livestock often thrived in the continental areas but struggled closer to the Mediterranean. And the cold weather conditions influenced the French to try many preservation methods, such as salting and smoking meat and boiling fruits, nuts, and many vegetables in honey. Salted fish, such as carp, pike, bream, eel, and tench, was also popular, as were the meats of ocean-going mammals such as whales and dolphins.

All of these influences have created a diverse array of dishes, such as *soupe à l'oignon*, a soup made of onions and beef stock; coq au vin, made of chicken flavored with wine and topped with mushrooms, salty bacon, onions, and garlic; beef bourguignon, a delicious stew of beef flavored with red wine, garlic, fresh herbs, and mushrooms; chocolate soufflé, a fluffy dessert that is popular around the world; and baked goods such as baguettes, *tarte tatin* (apple tart), and chocolate mousse.

WINE: A STAPLE OF NEARLY EVERY EUROPEAN MEAL

A glass or two of wine with a meal is an absolute must in most parts of Europe. A variety of factors drive the wild popularity of wine in Europe. First of all, in countries such as Italy and France—where the temperatures were warm enough—grapes flourished, and wine quickly spread throughout the continent. The comforting tastes and soothing sensations familiar when downing a glass of wine have made it a favorite digestive aid throughout the continent.

The popularity of wine (and beer in some parts of the continent) also peaked during the struggles of the Dark Ages and even throughout the Renaissance. During this time, water was unsafe to drink because filtering methods had not yet been invented. The preparation of beer and wine—and their preservation—made them safer alternatives to water. And while the importation of coffee during the Renaissance made it a staple of many diets, wine has remained the most popular meal drink throughout the continent.

Laborers pick and harvest grapes for winemaking in Tuscany, Italy.

SPAIN: A BLEND OF OLD AND NEW WORLD INFLUENCES

The cuisine of Spain has changed profoundly over the many centuries of its development. For example, the country once comprised three territories, divided into three clans: the Celts, who fished and farmed; the Iberians, who hunted and kept cattle; and the Tartessos, who traded mostly with Africa and Greece for foodstuffs. Under the Roman Empire, the country was united into one uneasy alliance, which was influenced during the Middle Ages by the Visigoths, who brought beer, sugarcane, spinach, lemon, and almonds into the area.

And when Spain "discovered" America in 1492, the Spanish imported many of its most delicious foods, such as spicy peppers, potatoes, tomatoes, vanilla, and chocolate. That's why traditional Spanish dishes like gazpacho (tomatoes, olive oil, garlic, and peppers) and *tortilla española* (eggs, potatoes, and onions) use so many ingredients that aren't native to the country. Paella (chicken, rabbit, saffron, and rice) and *tostas de tomate y jamón* (roasted ham scrubbed with garlic and tomato), meanwhile, do use more traditional Spanish ingredients.

A small village in the mountains of Almeria, Spain, holds an annual event where paella is made to feed an estimated 1,000 people.

New World Foods That Are Now Beloved in Europe

Although it is true that Europeans brought a large amount of food to the Americas when they settled there, New World foods came back to the Old World as well. Many of these foods have become staples of European dishes and have supplanted, or even replaced, some traditional meals. Potatoes, for example, were imported from Peru as early as the 1500s and quickly spread throughout the continent. In fact, some have argued that the easy-to-grow and nutritious potato helped fuel the European empires of the time.

Other foods, such as sunflower seeds, corn (maize), cacao (chocolate), tomatoes, squash, bananas, tobacco, and pineapples all originated in the New World. In some cases, particularly with the "Banana Wars" of Central America, these discoveries led to dire consequences. Imagine a world where tobacco had never been imported into Europe (or other regions) to cause untold health problems and deaths. However, this food swapping mostly benefited the continent and its cuisine.

Potatoes were unknown in Europe before they were imported from Peru beginning in the 1500s.

GREECE: A GLORIOUS MIXTURE OF EUROPE AND THE MIDDLE EAST

Greece may be the birthplace of democracy, but it also originated a unique and exciting cuisine style. Historically,

Many Greek meals include olives, feta, a mix of vegetables, and sometimes, octopus.

Western European, Middle Eastern, and North African cultures all influenced this small country's cuisine. The Greek Orthodox Church also promoted many changes in Greek food, including limitations on pork and meat during specific fasting periods like Lent.

These cultural influences mixed with ancient Greek recipes to create dishes like moussaka (fried eggplant, minced meat, and potatoes), *fasolatha* (white bean soup with tomatoes, onions, carrots, and celery), and *koulouri* (bread rings covered in sesame seeds), along with ingredients like olives, feta cheese, and more. Olives and feta come from the days of ancient Greece and were often used in various medical treatments.

The full English breakfast with eggs, bacon, sausage, toast, beans, and tomatoes.

ENGLISH CUISINE: NOT JUST BEANS ON TOAST

According to jokes and cliché (including from the English themselves), traditional British food is terrible. One thinks of this cuisine as "quirky" and influenced profoundly by the harsh weather conditions and sometimes poor growing soil common throughout the British Isles. Other influences on British cuisine include the need for quick-to-prepare meals that farmers and traders could eat while on the go.

In fact, however, over the last 30 years or so, British has gone from being the butt of many jokes to being one of the hottest cuisine styles in the world. For example, chefs like Gary Rhodes are reinvigorating English food by bringing in outside influences—like lobster from Asian countries—and combining it with British favorites, such as fried eggs. And celebrity chefs like Gordon Ramsay have brought traditional British pub cooking out of the isles and into the rest of the world.

SCANDINAVIA: CUISINE THAT WILL SOON BE COOL

In Sweden, surströmming, a fermented Baltic Sea herring, is a popular snack. The fermentation process makes it one very pungent mouthful.

The Nordic countries—Norway, Denmark, Sweden, Finland, and even Iceland—have survived some of the harshest weather conditions in Europe and created incredible cuisine styles. The sea-bound nature of these nations has led to some delicious fish meals, though elk, reindeer, and even bear meat are widespread throughout the region. A few familiar dishes in the area include cod baked with mustard sauce, dried stock-fish (unsalted cod dried by cold air and wind), minced pork and meatballs, cloud-berry sauce, rich fish porridges, and smoked horseflesh served between buns and called "hamburgers." Simplicity is often crucial, because traditional Nordic culture centered on hunting and gathering and staying mobile.

Arancini are filled with rice, cheese, and sometimes meat.

WHO DOESN'T LOVE ITALIAN CUISINE?

Like many people, you might think that Italian cuisine is nothing but pasta and pizza. If so, you couldn't be more wrong. Yes, pasta and pizza form a large portion of the traditional Italian diet. However, the Mediterranean influence on the region as a whole has had a powerful effect on Italian cuisine as well, expanding the dishes one finds here far beyond the traditional fare the country is known for.

For example, dishes like arancini (stuffed rice balls) and osso buco *alla Milanese* (tender veal served in white wine with vegetables) provide a welcome respite from pasta dishes in Italy. And for those who love meat, prosciutto and *ribollita*, a Tuscan vegetable and bread soup, can be combined to create a delicious pasta alternative.

CHAPTER 4 LATIN AMERICA AND THE CARIBBEAN

The cuisine of Latin America is as delicious as it is healthy and diverse. With rich contributions from countries like Mexico and Peru, as well as the many islands of the Caribbean, the foods created in this region are delicious, unique, and unforgettable.

EATING IN THE CARIBBEAN IS ABOUT MORE THAN FISH

As you can imagine, the many islands that make up the Caribbean rely heavily on ocean-caught fish. Most residents are likely to eat fresh fish multiple times every day. However, one shouldn't assume that every meal is baked, fried, or boiled fish, shrimp, crab, or lobster. Caribbean cuisine is incredibly diverse and features influences from a multitude of different continents.

For example, the Caribbean Islands were "discovered" by the Spanish in 1493 when Christopher Columbus landed there. The Spaniards brought along a variety of foods and foodstuffs, including coconuts, cilantro, eggplant, and garlic. However, other countries fought over the area for centuries, thanks to the unique strategic influence it had on the region. As a result, East Indian, Middle Eastern, Asian, and even African influences can be found in the average Caribbean dish.

The resourceful natives of the islands synthesized all of these cultural influences with their own, including ingredients like beans, bell peppers, tomatoes, sweet potatoes, coconut, and even rice. These ingredients go into a distinct marinade known as mojo. Smothering food with this mixture of garlic, onions, and

A man cooks Jamaican jerk over an open flame.

herbs gives Caribbean food its uniquely potent flavor. Many of these herbs and ingredients provide health benefits as well, including high concentrations of vitamins and minerals.

Paired with these vegetables and herbs are chicken and many types of fish. Chickens are a popular form of livestock on the Caribbean islands, because they are smaller and take up less room than cattle or pigs. Chicken dishes, such as Jamaican jerk, are fast becoming staples of Caribbean food fanatics around the world. Seafood such as rock lobster, crayfish, shrimp, and even conch snails appear in a variety of stews, salads, and soups across the islands.

Alongside these protein sources, beans, legumes, root vegetables, rice, and more are prepared using a unique cooking method that minimizes oil and butter use. Traditional Caribbean cooking methods include wood-fueled fires and many barbecue styles. For example, Jamaican barbecue cooking—known as barbacoa—consists of metal drums suspended over a fire. Ingredients are placed inside these drums and cooked for several hours. This method, called "coal stove cooking," often used charcoal as the heating element, due to its prominence on the island.

Most dishes prepared in these drums combine meat, vegetables, and legumes to create a wholesome and healthy dish that many in the Caribbean consider sacred. First, meat is added to the drums and, as it stews, the meat juices are collected and later spread over the top of a meal, like a gravy. Combined with fried yucca fritters, these meals are delicious and filling. Indeed, just reading about them is likely to induce hunger.

Fried yucca fritters.

WHY CENTRAL AMERICAN FOODS ARE EASY TO PREPARE

Few regions experience the kind of extreme heat that is common in Central America. Unfortunately, that heat makes cooking very hard for residents of the region. When dealing with the tangle of the many Central American jungles, most simply don't have the time to prepare elaborate dishes that require lengthy cooking times. Hence, most Central American dishes are relatively easy to make.

Just think of how easy it is to make tacos, for example. One only has to brown meat (or beans) in a skillet, add some spices, and serve on soft tortillas with tomatoes, lettuce, or whatever vegetables are desired or handy. The handheld nature of tacos helped Central Americans stay mobile while eating, allowing them to tend to their fields or hunt any animals that they could find nearby.

And like many areas of Latin America, European colonization influenced the region's cuisine. Many types of beans were imported to the area from Europe and became everyday staples. The rich refried beans common in countries like Mexico would not be possible

Tacos are small and easy to eat. People in Central America often eat them on the go.

without the influence of European culture. However, native Latin American cuisine has mostly been untouched for centuries and has developed in its own way.

That's why you can eat delicious *pupusa* from many street vendors across the area. Created in El Salvador, *pupusa* is a combination of freshly ground cornbread, bean paste, and cheese and is served warm. In Honduras, residents eat *baleadas* just about every day. These wheat flour tortillas are folded into a half-moon shape and stuffed with refried beans, sour cream, and cheese. Adding scrambled eggs creates an excellent breakfast.

In spite of stiff competition, though, few street foods are as popular as tamales. Wrap beef, rice, corn, peppers, and other ingredients in a plantain leaf, heat it up, and you have yourself a quick on-the-go snack that is both delicious and healthy.

A cook prepares pupusas at a pupuseria in El Salavador.

SOUTH AMERICAN CUISINE BORROWS (AND IMPROVES) ON MANY EUROPEAN TRADITIONS

Throughout history, many European countries have fought over, gained control of, and then left the South American region. These contentious battles have left a significant imprint on the population, including influencing their native cuisine. Although Spain and Portugal may have left the biggest impression on the area, there are many traditional recipes available throughout the continent.

For example, Europeans brought animals like cows, goats, pigs, and chickens to the region. Since then, livestock has had a significant influence on South American cooking. Other foods brought to the area include citrus trees, wheat, almonds, and more. Once these ingredients reached South American shores, though, each contributed to a unique mix that cannot be found anywhere else in the world.

Humitas are typically made with corn, onions, and various spices. The dough is wrapped in a corn husk and then boiled or baked.

Take the Andes region of South American as an example. This mountainous region was the least affected by European settlement and cuisine. As a result, foods such as corn, potatoes, and tubers are more common here than elsewhere on South America. Meat preferences here include llama and the guinea pig, along with trout and sea fish. Native peppers combined with these ingredients make up dishes like *humitas*, *arepas*, and *quimbolitos*.

By contrast, the Atlantic coastal regions of South America were the most influenced by European settlement. Here you'll find dishes prepared with grains, rice, wheat, and potatoes, such as *pabellon criollo*, and *sopa paraguaya*. The tropical Pacific and Amazon regions serve similar types of dishes but with a more native than European touch.

Pabellon criollo *is made with rice, plantains, and beans.*

That said, some areas of Brazil are more African-influenced and include dishes made from turtles, peccary, and other types of local meat.

Lastly, the Pampas region has a heavy influence from Italy and Germany, thanks to the European settlement cycle. Here you can find dishes like Argentina pizza, which is flavored and shaped like a calzone, and Spanish tortillas mixed with potatoes and meatballs.

NATIVE CULTURE REMAINS A POWERFUL INFLUENCE

European culture may hold considerable sway over large portions of Latin America, but the Native American culture remains a proud one. In Latin America, the native population irrigated their crops, created terraced growing areas on mountains, and even learned how to acclimate foods to regions in which they were not likely to grow. This agricultural knowledge remains strong throughout the area and continues to influence the new variations of food coming out today.

For example, the Inca people were so good at growing foods like corn, lima beans, sweet potatoes, peanuts, cacao, potatoes, and avocados that they almost never experienced starvation. And most of these ingredients (mainly corn and potatoes) remain critical elements of the Latin American diet. Therefore, it isn't uncommon to see Latin Americans enjoying a bowl of quinoa flavored with local peppers or even tropical fruits, such as mango and guava, while eating a European-style sausage. And while the Incan society unfortunately ceased to exist long ago, their intelligent growing methods (such as crop rotation) are still used throughout the area.

Peruvians still follow ways of the ancient Inca people, selling and eating grains like quinoa.

LLAMA MEAT: TRY IT, YOU MIGHT LIKE IT

Most Americans probably think of llamas as fun or exotic pets that their weird friends raise on farms. However, residents of South America have eaten llamas for over 5,000 years. That's longer than the domestication of most European meat sources. The Inca civilization, in particular, used llamas not only in their cuisine but also in religious rites. The Incans believed (correctly) that llama meat was healthy, and they wanted to provide their gods with only the healthiest meals.

Nowadays, llama meat dishes have spread throughout the rest of the world. Slightly gamey in texture and taste, it compares best to beef and lamb. Not quite as potent as lamb, llama does have more of a kick to it than beef. Exotic meat stores across the United States are starting to add llama meat to their stock, meaning that you could try it out for yourself if you were interested. After all, llama meat is both high in dense protein and low in cholesterol.

Llama tenderloin roasted on a hot stone.

THE ASIAN INFLUENCE ON LATIN AMERICAN FOOD

Tallarin saltado is made with locally grown vegetables and meats.

One might think that Latin America and Asia are worlds apart and that their cuisines wouldn't be related in any way. However, the Chinese Exclusion Act of 1882 in the United States caused Chinese laborers to immigrate to South America instead of North America. And even before that, Chinese immigrants made up at least 10 percent of the population of certain South American countries. And whenever they came to these lands, they brought their cuisines and food traditions with them.

As a result of this migration, dishes like *tallarin saltado* were born. This chow mein variant uses locally grown ingredients, including a multitude of seafood, to create a uniquely South American meal. Similar to Asian American cuisine, Asian Latin cooking has become famous throughout the continent.

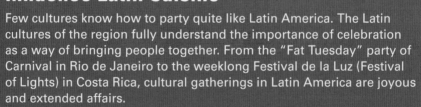

Carnival! How Cultural Celebrations Influence Latin Cuisine

Few cultures know how to party quite like Latin America. The Latin cultures of the region fully understand the importance of celebration as a way of bringing people together. From the "Fat Tuesday" party of Carnival in Rio de Janeiro to the weeklong Festival de la Luz (Festival of Lights) in Costa Rica, cultural gatherings in Latin America are joyous and extended affairs.

The influence these celebrations have on Latin cuisine is often quite subtle. For example, the hot and spicy nature of many of the region's foods is designed to create the feeling of fun and excitement felt at these festivals. The popularity of street food also originated at these parties, because celebrants want food that is quick to prepare and easy to carry.

HOW THE RAIN FOREST HAS INSPIRED LATIN AMERICAN CHEFS

Brazil nuts are used for many Latin American dishes.

Many areas of Latin America feature dense and life-giving rain forests. From this jungle environment, smart Latin American chefs have pulled inspiration for over a millennium. Even today, culinary experts are pulling together fresh rain forest ingredients and using them for incredible dishes. For example, Brazil nuts are commonly used in many Latin American entrées. And rain forest–derived ingredients, such as camu camu and acai, still inspire Latin American taste buds. In fact, experts estimate that thousands of undiscovered species of rain forest plants and animals may be found in the future, and some of them may be turned into the newest Latin American food fad.

Italian immigrants introduced gnocchi to Argentina.

LATIN AMERICAN DINING ETIQUETTE AND TRADITION

Dining traditions and etiquette vary in many ways around the world, including in Latin America. For example, although all countries have a tradition of saying a short prayer before eating, only in certain areas in Mexico do people cut their leftover or uneaten tortillas into pieces before throwing them away. In Argentina and Uruguay, meanwhile, gnocchi are eaten on the 29th day of every month. Such traditions are often unique to single countries, though some have spread throughout the region. For example, if someone pours wine or other drinks backward or with their left hand, they are telling the people they are serving that they dislike them.

A REGION RICH IN SPICY FOODS

Fans of spicy food often turn to Latin American cuisine to get their kicks. And who can blame them? With robust flavors as diverse as ancho (chili powder), chimichurri, chorizo bomb, Cuban spice, habanero, sassy steak spice, and cascabel chili to choose from, you'll never want for mouth-burning foods

Chimichurri, Argentina's spicy sauce.

in this part of the world. Mixing these spices with tacos, burritos, or even Asian Latin dishes will get a person's eyes watering and taste buds jumping. For those new to spicy food, or those who have a harder time stomaching these hot flavors, marinades or deseeded peppers serve as milder substitutes that still retain the tastes of the region.

BRAZIL'S TASTY CULINARY TREATS TANTALIZE THE TONGUE

As the largest country in South America, Brazil has had a significant influence on the culture of the continent. And the impact of Portugal and Spain—alongside its native dishes—make Brazil's cooking culture perhaps the most critical single influence on South America cuisine. It's here that you'll get the chance to enjoy delicious barbecue meats, *queijo coalho* (cheese on a stick), chicken hearts, soups (such as prawn and coconuts served with annatto seeds), *cachaça* (fermented sugarcane juice), *moqueca* (fish stew), and *brigadeiros* (delicious chocolate truffles). You might also try a popular street food called *acarajé*, which is a deep-fried patty made from black-eyed peas, onions, shrimp, and cashews.

Brigadeiros *are a wonderful* chocolate treat in Brazil.

CHAPTER 5 THE MIDDLE EAST

The Middle East sits in an exciting and turbulent part of the world. Those living here are not entirely Asian, European, or African but instead take influences from each of these continents. They use these traditions and influences—along with their own cultural and religious beliefs—to create an incredible cuisine tradition that should be on the plates of foodies around the world.

THE MIDDLE EAST: A MELTING POT OF CULINARY CULTURES

The lengthy history of invasions, religious crusades, and dictatorships in the Middle East is too long and complex to touch on here. Without going into much depth, it is worth knowing that influences from Jewish, Armenian, Turkish, Iranian, Assyrian, Kurdish, and Arab cultures are found in the taste profiles of many dishes in the Middle East.

The sometimes friendly and often rocky relationships among these cultures haven't stopped the spread of various foodstuffs over the years. For example, many Middle Eastern cultures were born around the Tigris and Euphrates Rivers and spread outward from this life-giving area. As a result, many Middle Eastern regions share an affinity for foods that grow in this region, such as grain, barley, pomegranates, dates, pistachios, and figs. Beer and bread were also first created in this area, which is why they figure so prominently in most cuisine types.

A familiar sight in the Middle East is charcoal-roasted lamb.

However, the invasion of the Mongolian Empire throughout the region also spread foods such as garlic, cumin, peppercorns, tomatoes, and more. Common elements such as wheat, rice, couscous, bulgur, butter, dried fruits, cinnamon, cloves, lamb, mutton, kebabs, *turşu*, cabbage, spinach, turnips, and eggplant unite Middle Eastern cuisine traditions above and beyond their many differences.

Turkish cuisine, for example, combines elements from the country's shared Middle Eastern tradition, incorporating influences from Eastern Europe, the Balkan states, and Central Asia. Expect a lot of rice, light use of spices and herbs, a rich variety of delicious vegetable stews, eggplants, fish, and meat fried on a kebab. The lighter use of spices makes Turkish cuisine one of the milder Middle Eastern cuisine styles.

In contrast, Jewish cuisine focuses heavily on vegetables, fruits, and meats that are considered kosher or clean. Therefore, all meat must be prepared according to strict Jewish law, meaning it must be drained entirely of blood, soaked in water for half an hour, and heavily salted before cooking. Meat and poultry cannot touch or be prepared with the same utensils as dairy products, meaning that feta-topped lamb would be out of the picture for those who follow kosher rules.

A vendor sells vegetables and fruit at a market in Jerusalem.

MIDDLE EASTERN GRAIN DISHES INSPIRED THE ANCIENT GRAIN FAD

Many people have recently added ancient grains to their diet. This fad is a healthy one, though the true believers may slightly exaggerate the benefits. However, eating these ancient grains is not a fad in the Middle East but rather a way of life. In fact, most of the ancient grains Westerners have come to love originated in Middle Eastern countries and remain staples in the region.

For example, bulgur (cracked wheat) is eaten throughout many areas of the Middle East. Bulgur salads provide a rich variety of flavor options, particularly when paired with tomatoes and an appropriate sesame-style sauce. The pre-cooked nature of bulgur makes it similar to pasta in the United States, because it can be warmed up in hot water to create a quick meal.

Bulgur salad.

Vinegar chicken over farro.

Farro (or emmer) is another favorite ancient grain eaten throughout the Mediterranean and the Middle East. High levels of fiber, iron, and protein make it an excellent choice for anybody trying to lose weight. Even better, farro requires very little preparation and can be cooked in half an hour. Squish it up into balls filled with tuna or other types of foods for a delicious and unique meal.

Kamut is a great ancient grain that originated in Egypt and has spread across the Middle East. Containing more protein and vitamin E than most grains, the copyrighted Kamut also possesses high levels of fiber. Dishes that go well with Kamut include pilafs, salads, and soups, or it can be served on top of a variety of meat dishes. It has a lengthier cooking time of about an hour, however, so these entrées take a bit longer to prepare.

These grain recipes are becoming popular because of their delicious taste and high fiber content. Most have fiber levels that are well beyond other grains, such as rice and quinoa. And grains like Kamut and farro have intense flavors that combine well with lamb and other types of meat dishes. Try out one of these grains to experience true Middle Eastern cuisine.

HOW RELIGION MADE LAMB A POPULAR MIDDLE EASTERN DISH

Anybody who has eaten at a Middle Eastern restaurant knows that lamb is a pre-ferred meat in this region. In fact, it is often hard to find dishes that include chicken, beef, or other types of meat. Religion is the most prominent factor in the popularity of lamb in the Middle East.

The two most prominent faiths in the area—Judaism and Islam—both pro-hibit eating pork. In addition, the kosher rules common in Jewish cuisine make it difficult to prepare these other meats suitably. Beyond that, lamb sacrifice is a common theme in both religions, giving lamb consumption considerable religious significance. Lamb dishes have therefore become diverse throughout the area.

A hearty lamb stew with chickpeas is enjoyed throughout the region.

Lamb cooked on skewers is often eaten with pita bread, hummus, and french fries.

For example, lamb stew is one of the main staples of many who live in the Middle East. This simple dish is made with olive oil, cumin, cayenne, salt, pepper, tomatoes, garlic, and a lamb broth. The broth is made by boiling large chunks of lamb in water, along with the other ingredients, and it is served while it is still warm. This dish may also be mixed with chickpeas and various types of vegetables to increase its health content.

Lamb pitas are also a favorite meal throughout the Middle East. These simple-to-prepare and handheld dinners consist of well-cooked lamb, feta cheese, onions, and many other ingredients. Pitas are another frequently featured Middle Eastern food, one that holds significant religious significance for both Judaism and Islam. Therefore, one can expect to see pitas paired with lamb and other popular favorites, such as hummus.

MIDDLE EASTERN CUISINE HIGHLIGHTS VEGGIES

Although lamb and grains are a staple of many Middle Eastern and Balkan countries, vegetables, especially pickled types, are just as important. Vegetable preparation methods vary, though frying is rare. Most countries prefer to boil, stew, stuff, or grill their vegetables and to pair them with meat and rice. Root vegetables, such as onions, carrots, turnips, garlic, and beets, are particularly widespread throughout the region. Grilling methods are frequently used throughout the area to minimize the heat spreading into in homes—after all, many Middle Eastern countries are in very warm regions.

Very rarely are vegetables eaten by themselves. Most Middle Eastern dishes combine them with meat and grains and cover everything with a meat-derived sauce. And though traditional plants remain a staple—because they are easiest to obtain—European and American vegetables, such as squash and tomato, are also integrated into many dishes. Many of these vegetables are important to Middle Eastern religions, particularly tomatoes. So, anticipate a lot of tomato and pepper flavoring whenever you eat a vegetable-oriented meal from the Middle East.

Tomatoes are integrated into many Middle Eastern dishes.

YOGURT—BORN IN THE MIDDLE EAST

Yogurt is a staple of many wellness-oriented diets and has become known as one of the healthiest of all meals. But did you know that it originated in the Middle East? The exact origin of yogurt isn't well known, but it popped up throughout the region about 6,000 years ago. The word *yogurt* is a Turkish term that means a thick and tart milk served cold.

When you understand yogurt production, its origin in the Middle East makes a lot more sense. Essentially, yogurt develops when milk is left to sit for an extended period. Healthy bacteria is introduced to the milk, which then invades the fluid and eats it, converting it into a thick and delicious fermented food product. The warm climates common throughout the Middle East made this bacteria easier to develop and likely increased the speed it took to work, which only hastened the discovery of this delightful and popular food.

Yogurt is always plentiful in the Middle East. This street vendor prepares a giant tub to sell.

EATING FROM THE SAME PLATE AS YOUR FRIENDS— AND USING YOUR HANDS!

Utensils are an uncommon sight in Middle Eastern countries. Many prefer to eat with their hands.

In most Middle Eastern countries, eating is done communally, meaning that one large plate of food is brought out, and everyone eats from that plate. Although each person may have a small plate on which to place their food, most people will be grabbing food directly from the large plate and eating it without utensils. This hand-to-mouth eating method may seem surprising to many utensil-bound cultures, but it has cultural significance due to the various religions in the region.

For example, many Hindus and Buddhists in the area believe that eating with your hands enhances your mind and spirit by keeping you connected to your food. Similarly, Muslim beliefs state that food should be eaten slowly and moderately and with the right hand. Like Hindus and Buddhists, Muslims believe that this enhances the eating experience. However, they are also following the eating patterns of the Prophet Mohammad, which is vital for their religious beliefs.

Religion Also Defines Middle Eastern Eating Etiquette

Eating with your hands may be strange to many Westerners, but it is far from the only way that Middle Eastern religions influence dining etiquette. For example, Jewish dining etiquette requires diners to avoid derogatory comments of any kind, especially toward the meal or the host's children, and to avoid unnecessary personal questions. Whispering is forbidden, because it is seen to be exclusionary and an attempt to hide your conversation from the group and from God.

Muslim dining etiquette follows similar concepts, including eating only allowed foods, which are known as *halal*. Saying "Bless Allah" is done before and after a meal. The right hand should be the only hand you eat with, because the left is considered evil. While eating, avoid excessive consumption and chew slowly to provide time to contemplate the origin of each piece of food.

HUMMUS: POPULAR IN THE MIDDLE EAST AND THE WEST

Hummus is made by crushing chickpeas.

The origin of hummus, a delicious favorite in the Middle East and elsewhere, has been debated heavily over the years. The first known mention of it was found in an ancient Egyptian cookbook from the 1200s. However, Greece and other Middle Eastern countries all claim that they invented it. Frankly, it doesn't matter who invented it, because many people are just glad that someone did. Indeed, Middle Eastern food wouldn't be the same without it. Whether used as a delicious dip for pitas and vegetables or as a topping for meat, this chickpea dip is a must-try staple for anybody interested in Middle Eastern cuisine.

Garlic is a staple ingredient in dishes found across the Middle East.

GARLIC: AN INGREDIENT WITH HEALING BENEFITS

Flip through any Middle Eastern cookbook, and you're going to find dozens of recipes that require garlic as an important ingredient. Traditional medicine throughout the Far East and the Middle East attributes a variety of healing properties to garlic, including managing wounds (because of its antiseptic properties) and improving heart health. It therefore also ends up in many dishes of the region. And though some of the more fantastical ideas about garlic have proven to be incorrect, science has shown that it does have many health benefits, including its use as an antibiotic, a source of high doses of vitamins like manganese, its virus-fighting capabilities, and its blood pressure management capability. Therefore, it's still a popular choice for Middle Eastern cooking to this very day.

MEAL ETIQUETTE: PRAISING YOUR GUESTS

Middle Eastern families gather together for a festive meal.

Whenever Middle Eastern families and friends get together for a large meal, the host is typically asked to give a speech. This tradition is part of many religious cultures and is done to praise friendship, the good wealth and health of everyone involved, and the food being consumed. Most speeches are performed during the meal, giving everyone the chance to enjoy some food beforehand. Concision and humbleness are emphasized. The host generally thanks his guests, those who couldn't show up, and God for the chance to enjoy a meal together. The host then waits for their guests to start the meal again before they resume eating.

A popular Jordanian dish, mansaf, is often topped with pine nuts for extra flavor and nutrition.

PINE NUTS: A FLAVORING YOU CAN'T GET IN THE NEW WORLD

The popularity of pine nuts is limited mostly to Europe, Asia, and particularly the Middle East. Afghanistan provides the region with many of these nuts, which are produced by trees like the Mediterranean stone pine, the single-leaf pinyon, and the chilgoza pine. Pine nuts are high in protein and vitamin B1, and they are useful as a flavoring on salads and meat dishes, or as a snack. Although pine nuts are available in America, they have yet to experience the same high level of popularity universal throughout the Old World. Most health food stores and supermarkets should have pine nut options from which you can choose.

CHAPTER **6** NORTH AMERICA

North America is a large part of the New World, and it has influenced cuisine around the world in a variety of ways. However, it has mostly adapted concepts from other cultures to create a unique and specific style of cooking. That said, Native American cuisine cannot be ignored in this relatively new culture of food preparation.

NATIVE AMERICAN CUISINE: A NEGLECTED ELEMENT IN AMERICAN COOKING

Before talking about U.S. Canadian, or Mexican food, Native American cuisine must be mentioned first. Few areas of the continent have been untouched by the cuisine culture of its indigenous peoples. These customs and foods have been exported to various parts of the world, including Europe and Asia, and have created many new styles of cooking. Native American food can be broken down by cultural regions. Northeastern Native American cooking focuses heavily on corn, beans, and squash. Historically, when planted together, these three staples would protect each other against insects and fungus, earning them the name "the Three Sisters." Eastern tribes cultivated plants such as amaranth, sumpweed, barley, maygrass, and sunflowers.

Southeastern Native American cuisine shares some traits with those of northern tribes. There was traditionally a lot of corn in these cultures, particularly when

Native Americans focused on hunting, cooking, and eating fish because it was plentiful in the rivers and lakes.

ground up to make a simple beer, and foods such as tomatoes, squash, pumpkins, and beans were also common. Peppers and sassafras were critical for their culture. And like all Native American cultures, many of these foods were considered sacred and believed to have healing properties.

By contrast, the peoples of the Great Plains focused heavily on bison or buffalo meat for their diet. Their traditional cooking method was drying it in the sun to make a delicious jerky. This preservation method helped meat last for months instead of days. In addition, cranberries, blueberries, cherries, currants, and Saskatoon berries were gathered and used to provide a multitude of health benefits.

Western Native American cultures tended to focus on fish, due to the prevalence of rivers and lakes and the proximity of the Pacific Ocean. Seaweed was often combined with vegetables such as mushrooms, berries, and various root vegetables. However, agriculture was not as common here because of the warmer climate and the abundance of meat. That said, acorns were one of the staple foods of Western native peoples.

These influences contributed to the development of foods we enjoy today, such as cornbread, succotash, bean bread, beef jerky, chili, cornmeal cakes, various types of teas, bean-oriented dishes (which spread into Mexico), casabe, hot chili peppers, pepperpot, tamales, and maple syrup.

Succotash.

THE US "MELTING POT" HAS CREATED WILDLY DIVERGING CUSTOMS

The United States calls itself the great "melting pot" of democracy. Within its borders, Native American, European, Middle Eastern, Asian, South American, Australian, and various religious cultures have combined to form one large, mixed country. Therefore, it is often hard to define North American cuisine, because it reflects so many cultures.

European cuisine is probably the most common influence for many in the nation. Here you can anticipate three meals a day, including heavy doses of meat and potatoes. However, the American tradition of eating the most substantial meal at dinner differs from the European lunch preference. The nine-to-five work schedule that is common throughout the country contributes to this focus on later meals.

Corn on the cob is one of the most popular items at a summer barbeque. You can thank the Native Americans for learning how to tame and grow this plant.

Are you a fan of nachos? You can thank the hardy settlers of Texas for inspiring these.

That said, this tradition is breaking up in many homes as people learn the health benefits of eating several smaller meals a day.

Even if Europe has the most substantial influence on US cooking, the tweaking of various traditions changed it profoundly over the years. For example, barbecue sauce and watermelon were brought over by enslaved Africans who were integrated into various areas of the country, particularly in the South. And Asian cooking has been transformed so much by American tastes that it can only be called Asian American.

That said, whether or not we realize it, the Native American influence is never far from the surface in the average U.S. diet. Do you eat corn with meals? You wouldn't if Native Americans hadn't learned how to domesticate it. Are you a fan of baked beans? Native cultures learned how to cultivate and cook beans hundreds of years before the European settlement of the continent.

And if you are a huge fan of Mexican cooking, Native Americans have a lot to do with its development. However, the grand European cuisine tradition in the nation often takes the "ethnic" edges off of these foods to create unique variations. For example, Tex-Mex food originated when the hardy settlers of Texas gave traditional Mexican food more spice.

MEXICO CITY: A CULTURAL MECCA OF CHANGING CUISINE CULTURE

Mexican food is not a static combination of tacos, burritos, and tamales. In fact, Mexican cuisine is continually changing and bringing in new outside influences. Mexico City is the best place to track these changes. As the capital of and largest city in Mexico, it provides both travelers and residents with the chance to experience an ever-changing variety of cuisines.

Mexico City is so critical to Mexican life that it has become a collection of all of the various cuisine cultures around the vast nation. For example, you can find traditional foods prepared in the Baha California area—which is influenced by trade between the nearby U.S. state of California and the Mexican state of Durango. Many of these more rural areas provide an interesting twist on traditional cuisine mixed with outside sources.

Vendors sell a wide variety of seafood and fruits and vegetables in Mexico City, one of the world's great culinary capitals.

Mole sauce is typically made with fruit, chili pepper, nuts, and various spices.

Mexico City also provides both residents and visitors with a high concentration of imported foods. Tropical fruits, various types of fish, and Asian rice are all imported into this great city. From here, shoppers take these foodstuffs home and use them to transform traditional Mexican cooking into something new and exciting.

Anybody walking through the streets of the city will experience one of the best street cuisine cultures in the world. Yes, you can chow down on delicious tacos, which are completely authentic, and experience what Mexican cooking is all about. However, you can also enjoy *birria, cabrito, carnitas,* mole sauces, and other types of haute cuisine found in many internationally renowned restaurants.

Regional differences will limit access to these foods outside of Mexico City. For example, *birria* is a Western Mexico dish that is hard to find in the East, while *cabrito* is practically nonexistent outside of the North. However, Mexico City collects this country's grand culinary traditions in one spot and provides them with the chance to influence each other in unique ways.

MEAT AND POTATO DISHES ARE NOT JUST A U.S. TRADITION

Anybody who lives in the United States has undoubtedly eaten a meal of meat and potatoes. This tradition extends to many individuals' ancestors, particularly from their farming days. It was often easier to eat nothing but meat and potatoes because both were easy to prepare and preserve. However, the meat and potatoes meal is not unique to the North American continent. In fact, most meat and potato dishes originated in Europe hundreds of years before immigration to America.

A quick trip to any country will showcase similar combinations, such as such as grilled lamb chops and mashed potatoes (Italy), hamburgers and fries (Germany), pork and baked potatoes (Spain), and even fish and chips (Great Britain). These dishes use ingredients common to each country and vary them to meet local taste. And integration of these dishes spread rapidly across the continent and was influenced by Native American traditions. For example, refried beans and french fries take the European tradition and add a uniquely New World flavoring and style.

Meat loaf and mashed potatoes is a classic American meal.

CANADIAN CUISINE: THE UNJUSTLY FORGOTTEN COUSIN

Although Canadian cuisine may not be as well known as U.S. and Mexican styles, some unique traditions here are worth knowing. Like U.S. cuisine, Canadian food has been influenced by its indigenous peoples, by European settlement, and even by the cuisines of Asia. The ways that Canadians have combined these influences, however, varies slightly from their southern cousins.

For example, due to the influence of native cultures, maple syrup is one of the most prominent staples of the country. Likewise, many areas skip beef or chicken jerky and favor a salmon jerky, first created by indigenous peoples across the region. The Russian impact on the area is also surprisingly significant—many people eat vegetables derived from Russia, such as cabbage, celery, and basil. And the Asian influence, which comes mostly from China, has variations much like Asian American food. Here's a fun fact: The "Chinese buffet" that has become so popular in the United States actually originated in Gastown, Vancouver, in the late 1800s.

Maple syrup isn't just for pancakes and waffles! In Canada, maple syrup is poured over snow and rolled into lollipops.

NORTH AMERICAN SPICES PROVIDE A UNIQUE CONTRAST TO OLD WORLD HERBS

A farmer picks fresh vanilla bean pods.

Most of the spices eaten in North American cuisine come from the Old World. In fact, only three spices are native to North America: allspice, capsicum peppers, and vanilla. These spices provide a unique contrast to European, Asian, and African spices, and they became wildly popular during the early days of American settlement. European settlers who were used to peppers from India started using capsicum peppers heavily in their dishes.

However, North America has provided a significant number of culinary herbs to world cuisine. Wild mint and horsemint originated on this continent and offer a sharp, but fresh, minty taste. Sagebrush, juniper, and wild onion grow throughout most of the continent. These herbs are not only considered tasty but are also used in many Native American healing traditions. Other healing herbs include loveroot, California bay, and tarragon. These healing herbs are still sold in various parts of the United States in health food shops, and even in supermarkets.

Oaxaca: The Culinary Capital of Mexico?

Although the influence of Mexico City on the culinary traditions of the country cannot be overstated, there is a good chance that Oaxaca is just as important—if not more so. Oaxaca is the capital city of the same-named state and is one of the most important cities in the country. Its southern location makes it more mountainous than the rest of the nation, which has contributed to its unique culinary traditions.

For example, Oaxaca was the first area of the country to cultivate corn and beans. Beyond that, it first domesticated cacao, used to make chocolate, and it also created mescal, a popular alcoholic beverage made from agave. Mescal is used today to create drinks like tequila and remains a potent alcoholic option. And if you're a fan of mole sauces, almost all of them originated in Oaxaca. Many food fanatics take pilgrimages to this city to experience its diverse and unforgettable combination of foodstuffs.

THE UNITED STATES HAS INFLUENCED MANY CUISINES AROUND THE WORLD

The increased cultural prominence of the United States, starting in the early 1900s, has inspired interesting cross-cultural cuisine sharing. For example, foods that originated in other countries—like the hamburger—were tweaked by American tastes and then exported to other countries. McDonald's and other fast-food

Although it may not be the "best" pizza in the United States, places like Pizza Hut and Domino's have created several variations of the classic Italian dish.

restaurants have popularized the hamburger in Asian nations. Although Asian chefs have tweaked the hamburger recipe in many ways, the basic style remains the same. And pizza giants like Little Caesars and Pizza Hut have taken this Italian dish and forever changed it. Some call this a degradation of the tradition, whereas others consider it an expansion, but there's no getting away from the influence of U.S. culture.

New York City hot dogs can be found on almost every street corner.

ON-THE-GO AMERICANS LOVE THEIR HANDHELD FOODS

No matter where you live in North America—from New York City to Ottawa to Tijuana—the constant "on-the-go" culture so prevalent in much of the continent has influenced the way that people eat. The popularity of simple handheld foods, such as hot dogs, pizza, and tacos, has rapidly spread throughout many cities. As a result, street foods have become one of the most popular dining choices in large cities. Residents stand in line for just a few moments to get a tasty (but not always healthy) meal. Many believe that this reliance on cheap food is contributing to obesity rates, however.

FOOD TRUCKS ARE TRANSFORMING THE BAR SCENE IN UNEXPECTED WAYS

Food trucks line the street in New York City.

Though food trucks have been around for decades, their increased popularity in the twenty-first century has created a renaissance of unique culinary options. However, many of these trucks tend to park near bars, because many hungry—and sometimes drunk—customers are likely to show up. The bar scene on the North American continent has always been rather wild, but food trucks add a whole new element. Instead of taking a taxi home and eating warmed-up leftovers after a night on the town, people can now eat real chow mein, plump hot dogs, or even sushi from a food truck. Food trucks might even help with some bad alcohol consumption decisions, because eating food absorbs alcohol in the stomach and minimizes its mental impact.

Shrimp gumbo.

CAJUN COOKING: A WEIRD AND WILD NORTH AMERICAN CUISINE

Cajun cuisine is one of those traditions that could have originated only in North America. Although it is based on a French style of cooking, derived from French Canadians who later settled in the region around New Orleans, it is also influenced by native cuisine and is specific to a region of the United States that has access to particular ingredients—namely, the bayou areas of southern Louisiana, with its rich seafood stores and access to aromatic vegetables. A typical Cajun gumbo will be made with shrimp or crawfish, mixed with onions, celery, dried cayenne pepper, bay leaf, and more. Ingredients are cooked using a variety of methods, including barbecuing, baking, and charbroiling. The result is something you can't get in any other part of the world.

CHAPTER 7 OCEANIA

Oceania is a vast collection of islands that stretch as far north as Hawaii and as far south as the continent and country of Australia. Island nations in this region, such as Papua New Guinea, New Caledonia, and the Solomon Islands, possess a unique and unforgettable collection of cuisines that will make you hungry for more.

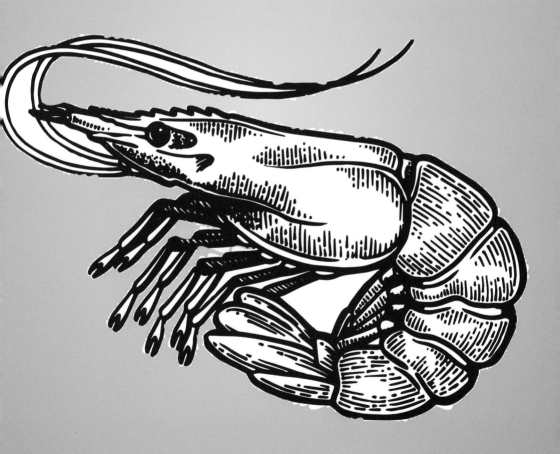

AUSTRALIAN CUISINE: MUCH MORE THAN "SHRIMP ON THE BARBIE"

Australia is an exciting place. For one thing, it is the only continent that is also a nation. Interestingly, about 80 percent of its population lives no more than 30–50 miles away from the ocean. And because European settlement here is relatively new, the Aboriginal peoples of the area had full control over the cuisine culture for roughly 40,000 to 60,000 years prior to the colonial era.

When the inevitable clashes between European and native cultures occurred, there was still a large amount of cuisine-swapping happening. For example, foods such as kangaroo, emu, bush berries, fruits, and different kinds of honey inspired the settlers to alter their eating habits. In many cases, these additions to European diets were a necessity, because early colonists found themselves struggling to grow European crops in the sometimes harsh and unforgiving climate of the continent.

In fact, the initial diet of settlers featured such bland fare as bread, salted meat, and tea. After a few days with this paltry cuisine, most started hunting

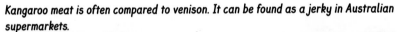

Kangaroo meat is often compared to venison. It can be found as a jerky in Australian supermarkets.

swans and geese, and catching fish, so they could eat a more diverse range of foods. Eventually, sheep were settled in the region and became one of the primary sources of food for Europeans. Vegetables and fruits such as bean shoots, cauliflower, mushrooms, tomatoes, squash, and asparagus finally took root in the area and became staples of many Australian diets.

Early British settlement of the continent ensured that tea and coffee became staples of the average Australian's diet as well. And dishes such as vegemite—a thick black spread made out of yeast and vegetable extracts—on toast follow the British tradition of putting something strange and delicious on a piece of bread. Barbecued shrimp remains a national favorite, as do meat pies, which are made with minced beef covered in beef gravy and cooked in a pastry shell. Sometimes kangaroo meat takes the place of beef in these pastries. Here's a fun fact: Australians are the only people who eat their national animal. Kangaroo meat is relatively gamey and thus similar to venison. In addition, lamb has become a trendy meat alternative for many.

Vegemite is typically spread on toast.

FIJI: FISH FEEDS AN ENTIRE NATION OF HUNGRY PEOPLE

Like many Pacific island nations, Fiji's history is one of much conflict. Initially settled by Melanesian people 3,500 years ago, the complex and well-developed society of Fiji caused problems for British settlers such as James Cook and William Bligh. Interestingly, early British rulers in the region worked with the native Fijians to protect their independence as a culture, which helped them prepare for true governmental autonomy in the 1960s. Their traditional cuisine culture, therefore, remained mostly intact and relatively uninfluenced by outside changes.

Coconuts are plentiful and often sold at the market.

Kokoda is a raw mackerel dish served in a coconut shell.

Coconuts and tubers—including taro—remain the staple of most Fijian diets. However, the Indian influence on Fiji—due to the importation of Indians as slaves in the early days of British rule—created subtle variations on many dishes. For example, cassava boiled in salt and water and eaten with curries comes mostly from the minds of the remaining Indian settlers. China has also had an influence on the island, particularly in its preparation and preference for seafood.

Fijian fish dishes vary depending on seasonal changes. entrées like *kokoda* (raw mackerel marinated in freshly squeezed lemon juice) pair well with roti, a bread covered with butter or jam. Black tea flavored with lemons is a typical drink accompanying most dinners. Thick stews made from chicken, fish, and root potatoes provide a traditional family meal that is served at many gatherings and religious rituals.

NEW ZEALAND LAMB IS A FAVORITE AROUND THE WORLD

In the eyes of many people around the world, New Zealand is the little sibling of Australia. However, the quirks of New Zealand culture led to a unique cuisine style. The most significant difference is likely its more substantial focus on raising and eating sheep. The cliché states that there are more sheep in New Zealand than there are people, and in Kiwi filmmaker Peter Jackson's earliest movie, *Bad Taste*, a (fake) sheep is blown up for a cheap gag. Bad jokes aside, New Zealand lamb is some of the best in the world.

Sheep farming did not become popular in the nation until the 1850s. The first attempt to raise sheep here was in 1773, and it failed miserably when the two

A New Zealand sheep herd.

introductory animals died within days of landing. Since then, nearly two centuries of breeding have created a smaller, but hardier, sheep that is capable of withstanding the uniquely harsh weather conditions of New Zealand.

In fact, New Zealand farmers send their sheep to other areas of the world as a source of meat and wool. And the average New Zealand diet consists of a large amount of lamb, particularly during the Sunday roast common for many families. During this meal, families eat a leg of lamb combined with roasted vegetables, such as potatoes, sweet potatoes, and peas. A glass of wine or beer typically helps to punctuate the meal with a flourish.

Variations on the basic roasted lamb chops include lamb meatballs, lamb steaks, and even stews that contain rich flavors created with native spices. Unique plants like kawakawa, pikopiko, and karengo create sharp flavors that are unique to New Zealand and produce a delicious and unforgettable cuisine culture.

Sunday (and Christmas) dinners often include a lamb roast, assorted vegetables, and wine or beer.

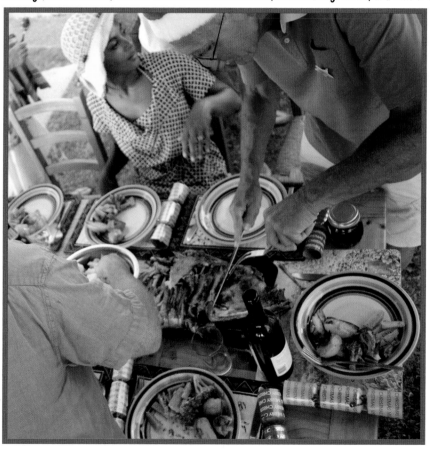

TASMANIA IS AUSTRALIAN FOR BEER

With all due respect to Foster's and its claim as *the* Australian beer, Tasmania may be Australia's most critical brewing force. Though small, this island state of Australia provides a vast majority of the beers sold and enjoyed in the country. In fact, it hosts the Taste of Tasmania Food and Beverage Festival every year, attracting over 250,000 people. During this event, various types of Tasmanian and Australian beers are shared with travelers from around the world.

Tasmanian beers include multiple types of IPAs (India pale ales) and richer English dark ales. Most compare well to German- and American-brewed beers, but they have unique taste profiles. For example, some breweries add native ingredients to their hops, such as various types of Australian berries. In this way, a unique and unforgettable brewing scene inspires locals and tourists alike. And the export of these brewed options is continuing to grow nearly every year.

A beer tasting at a Tasmania brewery.

TINY CHRISTMAS ISLAND PROVIDES AN ECLECTIC AND MEMORABLE CUISINE MIX

Although just 1,200 people live on this Australian settlement, a unique mixture of Chinese, Malaysian, and European cultures have created a cuisine unlike any other in the area. Although locally grown foods are rare due to a massive nematode infestation in the soil, community gardens throughout the nation provide a respite from the imported food that is a mainstay of the island. In this way, Christmas Island has learned to take care of most of its culinary needs without outside help.

Though Christmas Island shares some cuisine similarities with Australia, ingredients like papaya, coconut, chili, jackfruit, tapioca, and guava are popular here. Chickens provide a majority of meat in the area, and their pickled eggs are a favorite snack of many locals. Christmas Island meals combine these ingredients, including traditional fare such as lemon chili chicken or *roti canai*, a delicious bread that takes about eight hours to cook.

Roti canai is a delicious bread made on tiny Christmas Island. It is often eaten as a snack with meat and pickled eggs.

EARTHEN STOVES REMAIN A POPULAR PREPARATION METHOD

Imagine placing your food in the ground and cooking it in a large earthen stove. This method of cooking was prevalent for thousands of years in the Oceania region. And although modern and more convenient preparation methods are standard in more settled areas, indigenous people still prefer to use this method rather than gas or electric stoves.

Mostly, though, many stick with earthen stoves out of traditional preference. These stoves provide natives with a slow-cooking style that is unique to the area and offers many advantages,

Earthen stoves have been used for thousands of years in the Oceania region. Many people there still prefer them to modern stoves.

such as richer cooking juices. Some modern cooking methods may utilize similar slow-cooking concepts, but they don't create the same types of flavors common with the earthen stove. Therefore, strong tradition surrounds these ovens, including as using them to prepare foods—such as chicken and peppers—for specific holiday celebrations, such as various religion rites and coming-of-age rituals.

Fish Are a Critical Part of the Pacific Diet

The massive size of the Pacific Ocean influences the diet of just about every Oceania native. Fishing has provided them with food for thousands of years and remains a vital part of their survival. The fish in the area are diverse and offer many different taste options. For example, sardines, anchovies, Chilean horse mackerel, hake, and even squid provide both sustenance and commerce for residents.

More exotic fish, such as various species of tuna, create an incredible industry for the area. Hundreds of thousands of tons are caught in the area every year. Once processed, this tuna is canned and sent to supermarkets around the world. And residents of the area still enjoy catching these large fish, cleaning them, and smoking their meat for long-term preservation.

VARIED SETTLEMENT CYCLES AND EUROPEAN SETTLEMENT TRANSFORMED HAWAIIAN CUISINE

In Hawaii, people enjoy eating octopus flavored with tomatoes, onions, sesame oil, and chili pepper.

The earliest settlers of Hawaii were Polynesian sailors, who struggled to find many edible foods on the island and mostly ate taro, potatoes, and fish. As the island was continually "discovered" and settled by various other cultures, cuisine styles changed appropriately. For example, pigs and dogs were once the staple meats of most Hawaiians. Pineapple and sugarcane then became more important as European settlement expanded these industries. And the Asian influence—from China, Korea, and Japan—brought kimchi and rice to the islands. Combined with traditional dishes, such as *tako* (octopus flavored with tomatoes, onions, sesame oil, and chili pepper), a diverse and unpredictable variety of foods have been created for Hawaiians to enjoy.

A group of young boys search the shore for coconut crabs.

ISOLATION AND CONFLICT CONTRIBUTE TO A UNIQUE MARIANA ISLANDS CUISINE

The Mariana Islands consist of 16 different islands, 12 of which are unoccupied. A population of just over 200,000 mostly centers on Guam, though tensions dating back to World War II often make these islands hostile toward each other. Nevertheless, they have created a cuisine culture unique to their tiny population. Fresh fish from the ocean make up a majority of their meals. However, special rituals—including death rituals influenced by the imported Catholic religion common in the area—call for imported chicken and pork at times. To this day, native islanders eat more coconut crabs, octopus, shrimp, and fish than any other nation in the world. Flavorings for this meat include soy sauce, green onions, lemon juice, and crushed red pepper.

WHAT IS A BALMAIN BUG, AND WHY IS IT SO DELICIOUS?

Most people probably don't want to eat bugs for dinner. However, people around Oceania love eating the Balmain bug almost every day. But if you are thinking you would never eat a bug, don't worry—the Balmain bug is actually just a type of lobster. With a broad head and a flat body, it looks like a weird alien invader. However, these Balmain bugs (or bay lobsters) can be cooked just like crabs or crawfish. With sweet white meat that is easy to prepare and delicious to eat, the Balmain bug is one confectionery critter that you have to try if you ever make it to Australia.

Balmain bugs.

Purple yams.

BUSH TUCKER IS NOT A BAND

For a vast majority of the area's history, bush tucker (or bush food) provided sustenance for the native population in portions of Australia. Unique fruits and berries, such as quandong, muntries, riberry, and finger lime provided vitamins and minerals to a people who were always on the move and mostly hunting. The sharp taste of many types of bush tucker kept European settlers from enjoying them for centuries. Therefore, the native cuisine has remained mostly untouched by European influence. However, vegetables like the purple yam and round yam, and nuts like the sea almond and Australian cashew, remain staples of the region.

FURTHER READING & INTERNET RESOURCES

BOOKS

Allen, Nancy Krcek. *Discovering Global Cuisines: Traditional Flavors and Techniques*. London: Pearson, 2013.
In this book, you will learn more about traditional food preparation techniques. Many recipes (and the histories behind them) are explored in great depth.

Deetz, Kelley Fanto. *Bound to the Fire: How Virginia's Enslaved Cooks Helped Invent American Cuisine*. Lexington, KY: University Press of Kentucky, 2017.
This insightful book showcases the sacrifice that American slaves went through as food preparers. It also highlights how their influence transformed American food forever.

Civitello, Linda. *Baking Powder Wars: The Cutthroat Food Fight That Revolutionized Cooking*. Urbana, IL: University of Illinois Press, 2017.
Without baking powder (and the surprising history described in this book), many modern recipes would be impossible. Learn where baking powder comes from and the business history behind it.

Collingham, Lizzie. *The Taste of Empire: How Britain's Quest for Food Shaped the Modern World*. New York: Basic Books, 2017.
The British Empire spread a variety of foods around the world and created a unified world cuisine that changed history.

Fraser, Linda, and Sarah Ainley. *The Around the World Cookbook: Over 350 Authentic Recipes from the World's Best-Loved Cuisines*. London: Hermes House, 1999.
Learn how to prepare 350 authentic dishes from all around the world. This cookbook touches on recipe cultures from many different parts of the world.

Sherman, Sean, and Beth Dooley. *The Sioux Chef's Indigenous Kitchen*. Minneapolis: University of Minnesota Press, 2017.
This book provides a discussion of the impact of the Sioux Nation on America's cuisine culture. Includes multiple recipes that are easy to make and delicious.

WEB SITES

bbc.com/food. The food section of the BBC provides specialized recipes and exciting looks into the development of world cuisine.

cooking.nytimes.com. *The New York Times* cooking section provides detailed and delicious food options for the foodie in all of us.

epicurious.com. Learn more about modern and traditional cooking methods, various recipes, and the known history behind them.

foodmuseum.com. Explore the history of food, its development around the world, and various food heritage lessons on this insightful Web site.

nypl.org/node/5629. The New York Public Library's "Culinary History" page provides an extensive and enlightening look at the history of various culinary practices.

AUTHOR'S BIOGRAPHY

Eric Benac is a freelance writer with over 10 years of experience, including three years as a sports writer and two as a marketing specialist. He has won many awards, including a "140 Character" short story writing contest. He lives in Traverse City, Michigan, and loves electronic music.

COVER

(clockwise from top left) tortillas, Mexico City, Mexico, grandriver/iStock; Jerk chicken, London, England, AmyLaughinghouse/iStock; pastries, Marrakesh, Morocco, Matyas Rehak/Dreamstime; pizza, Rome, Italy, puntacristo/Shutterstock; sushi platter, StephanRocoplan; yams, Kalale, Benin, Cora Unk Photo/Shutterstock

INTERIOR

1, Gaus Alex/Shutterstock; 2–3, Dmitrii Sakharov/Shutterstock; 5, Dmitry Rukhlenko/Shutterstock; 9, Inked Pixels/Shutterstock; 10, Fanfo/Shutterstock; 11, yula/iStock; 12, Tanchic/iStock; 13, Sjors737/Dreamstime; 14, Auldist/Shutterstock; 15, Andrew Henn/Shutterstock; 16, Denis Gateau/iStock; 17, SilvaPinto1985/ iStock; 18, Bernardo Ertl/Dreamstime; 19 (UP), Wesley Lazarus/Shutterstock; 19 (LO), Pajac Slovensky/ Shutterstock; 20 (UP), pixzzle/iStock; 20 (LO), Alan_Lagadu/iStock; 21, Bukavik/Shutterstock; 23 (UP), chuyuss/Shutterstock; 23 (LO), Uwe Aranas/Shutterstock; 25 (UP), yumehana/iStock; 25 (LO), Vassamon Anasukkasem/Shutterstock; 26, Radiokukka/iStock; 27, Sitti/Shutterstock; 28, robertcicchetti/iStock; 29, Arisara T/Shutterstock; 30, xuanhuongho/Shutterstock; 31 (UP), Treetree2016/Shutterstock; 31 (LO), silentwings/Shutterstock; 32 (UP), Sahachatz/Shutterstock; 32 (LO), Phuong D. Nguyen/Shutterstock; 33, makar/Shutterstock; 34, frantic00/Shutterstock; 35, Corinna Haselmayer/Shutterstock; 36, pamuk/Shutterstock; 37, TatyanaNazatin/Shutterstock; 38, Meandering Trail Media/Shutterstock; 39, Alain Intraina/ iStock; 40, LaraBelova/iStock; 41, carpinxo/iStock; 42, Linda Williams/Dreamstime; 43 (UP), Andrei Bortnikau/Shutterstock; 43 (LO), mtreasure/iStock; 44 (UP), Multiart61/Dreamstime; 44 (LO), JannHuizenga/ iStock; 45, Sergio Bellotto/iStock; 46, Katyenka/Dreamstime; 47, Alexat25/Dreamstime; 48, Fotos593/ Shutterstock; 49, rj lerich/Shutterstock; 50, salmon-negro/Shutterstock; 51, Olaf Speier/Shutterstock; 52, Christian Vinces/Shutterstock; 53, Josip Matanovic/iStock; 54, Robin Hann/Dreamstime; 55 (UP), Paralaxis/iStock; 55 (LO), SC Image/Shutterstock; 56 (UP), Ildipapp/Dreamstime; 56 (LO), erikapellini/ iStock; 57, DiViArt/Shutterstock; 58, Lepneva Irina/Shutterstock; 59, Chalffy/iStock; 60, Brent Hofacker/ Shutterstock; 61, DebbiSmirnoff/iStock; 62, Alexander Mychko/Dreamstime; 63, Pipa100/Dreamstime; 64, Evgeniy Fesenko/Dreamstime; 65, Prometheus72/Shutterstock; 66, Sevenstock Studio/Shutterstock; 67 (UP), FrauTori/Shutterstock; 67 (LO), Fazlin Hafiz/Shutterstock; 68 (UP), Rawpixel.com/Shutterstock; 68 (LO), bonchan/Shutterstock; 69, Epine/Shutterstock; 70, davelogan/iStock; 71, Mix3r/iStock; 72, kali9/ iStock; 73, David Cabrera Navarro/Dreamstime; 74, NadyaRa/Shutterstock; 75, Larisa Blinova/Dreamstime; 76, Nathalie Speliers/Dreamstime; 77, PaulMcKinnon/iStock; 78, Veerasak Komsansai/Shutterstock; 79 (UP), ChameleonsEye/Shutterstock; 79 (LO), Sandra Foyt/Dreamstime; 80 (UP), Tupungato/Dreamstime; 80 (LO), LauriPatterston/iStock; 81, Alexander_P/Shutterstock; 82, Bundit Minramun/Dreamstime; 83, Ben185/iStock; 84, Carynn/Shutterstock; 85, ChameleonsEye/Shutterstock; 86, georgeclerk/iStock; 87, LazingBee/iStock; 88, Michael R Evans/Shutterstock; 89, Zull Must/Shutterstock; 90, Glen_Pearson/ iStock; 91 (UP), 400tmax/iStock; 91 (LO), RaksyBH/Shutterstock; 92 (UP), Jonathan Austin Daniels/iStock; 92 (LO), Wanida Larkjitr/Dreamstime